The Urbana Free Library

To renew: call **217-367-4057**
or go to **urbanafreelibrary.org**
and select **My Account**

Help Me Understand

What Happens at a Funeral?

David Crossmeister

PowerKiDS press™

NEW YORK

Published in 2019 by The Rosen Publishing Group, Inc.
29 East 21st Street, New York, NY 10010

First Edition

Editor: Elizabeth Krajnik
Book Design: Rachel Rising

Photo Credits: Cover © iStockphoto.com/kzenon; p. 4 Kamira/Shutterstock.com; pp. 5, 15 RichLegg/E+/Getty Images; p. 7 Quality Stock Arts/Shutterstock.com; p. 9 Richard T. Nowitz/Corbis Documentary/Getty Images; p. 10 sethislav/Shutterstock.com; p. 11 Syda Productions/Shutterstock.com; p. 13 Monashee Frantz/OJO Images/Getty Images; p. 16 Mega Pixel/Shutterstock.com; p. 17 Christopher Spahr/Shutterstock.com; p. 18 Funny Solution Studio/Shutterstock.com; p. 19 WHL/Blend Images/Getty Images; p. 20 Dieter Heinemann/Getty Images; p.21 Komwanix/Shutterstock.com; p. 22 Kasefoto/Shutterstock.com.

Cataloging-in-Publication Data

Names: Crossmeister, David.
Title: What happens at a funeral? / David Crossmeister.
Description: New York : PowerKids Press, 2019. | Series: Help me understand | Includes glossary and index.
Identifiers: LCCN ISBN 9781508167006 (pbk.) | ISBN 9781508166986 (library bound) | ISBN 9781508167013 (6 pack)
Subjects: LCSH: Funeral rites and ceremonies–Juvenile literature. | Death–Social aspects–Juvenile literature.
Classification: LCC GT3150.C76 2019 | DDC 393–dc23

Manufactured in the United States of America

CPSIA Compliance Information: Batch #CS18PK: For Further Information contact Rosen Publishing, New York, New York at 1-800-237-9932

Contents

A Fact of Life

All living things will die someday. Plants, animals, and people die when they're old. Many people live for a long time, but some people die when they're younger.

When someone dies, it's usually a sad, confusing, and scary time for that person's family and friends. A funeral is a special **ceremony** that helps make a person's death easier for their family and friends to accept. Going to a funeral may sound scary, but it can be a special time to celebrate the life of a loved one who has passed away.

The death of a family member can be very upsetting, especially for children. Families help each other deal with the loss.

5

A Time to Grieve

Funerals are an important part of the **grieving** process. Grieving the death of a loved one is natural and healthy. However, it's not healthy to go through it alone. Funerals offer families a chance to gather and **honor** the person who died.

Different groups of people have different funeral **traditions**. No matter what your traditions are, funerals allow people to take the time to remember a person's life. They also help friends and family learn to accept that someone they love is no longer with them.

During traditional Chinese funerals, friends and family members burn special paper, fake money, and paper figures. This is to help the person who passed away have a safe journey to the **afterlife**.

Religious Service

Funerals are most often held in a religious place, such as a church, temple, or mosque. People going to a funeral usually wear formal clothes. This is a sign of respect for the person who died.

Many funerals are religious services. A religious leader may say a prayer and talk about the person who died. Often, a funeral includes a eulogy. This is when someone close to the person who died talks about their life in front of those attending.

Funerals are part of most religions. Each religion has special words, actions, and songs performed during a funeral.

Funeral Home

Not all funerals take place in a religious location. Some are held in a special place called a funeral home. The first thing you may notice when you arrive at a funeral home is a big box made of wood or metal. This is the casket. The body of the person who died is kept in the casket.

At some funerals, the casket is open. You can get close to the person who died and say your last words to them if you want.

open casket →

Some funerals have closed caskets. It depends on the family and their traditions.

11

It's OK to Grieve

A funeral is a sad event. Don't be scared if you see your mom or dad or other grown-ups crying. Crying is a part of grieving. Grieving means accepting that a special person has died and is gone from your life. Grieving helps your mind sort through the sad, confusing feelings that happen when someone dies.

At a funeral, you grieve with others. Grieving helps people handle a death in the family. Sharing your pain with others in your family is a healthy way to grieve.

It's always unhealthy to keep your feelings to yourself. Talking about your feelings will help you feel better.

13

Going to the Cemetery

After the funeral service, the casket may be carried out of the building by the pallbearers. Pallbearers are usually family members or close friends of the person who died. They place the casket in a long car called a hearse.

Everyone at the funeral gets into their own cars and follows the hearse to the **cemetery**. This is called a funeral **procession**. Sometimes a police officer leads the funeral procession to make sure everyone gets to the cemetery safely.

Being a pallbearer is an honor. It's a very important job. However, some people may be too sad at a funeral to be a pallbearer.

At the Cemetery

You've probably seen a cemetery in your town or while riding in a car. A cemetery is a big, grassy place where people who have died are buried. You will probably see many **gravestones**. These mark the places where people are buried.

Gravestones usually show the person's name, their birth date, and their date of death. Some also have special sayings on them. Some gravestones are plain, and some are small. Some gravestones are fancy, and some are very big.

Cemeteries are quiet, beautiful, peaceful places where people can visit the graves of their loved ones.

17

Last Words

Once the funeral procession reaches the cemetery, the pallbearers carry the casket to the grave. A grave is a hole about 6 feet (1.8 m) deep. This is where the casket is laid to rest.

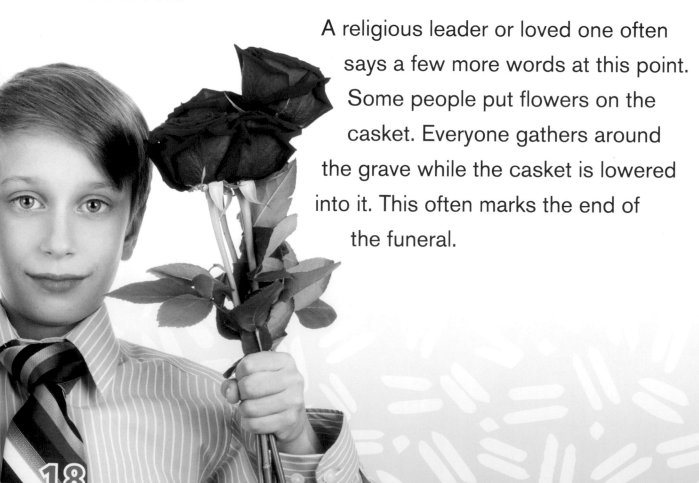

A religious leader or loved one often says a few more words at this point. Some people put flowers on the casket. Everyone gathers around the grave while the casket is lowered into it. This often marks the end of the funeral.

Once the funeral is over and people have left the cemetery, the grave is filled with dirt and grass is planted over it.

19

What Is Cremation?

While many traditions call for a burial after death, some people prefer cremation. This is when the body is burned in a place called a crematorium. After the body is cremated, all that's left is ashes. The ashes are usually placed in a small container called an urn.

Some families keep the urn in their home. Others bury it in a cemetery. Still others prefer to spread the ashes in a place that was special to the person who died.

decorative urn

Some urns are very plain, while others can be very fancy.

21

Remembering Your Loved One

Family members usually don't want to be alone after a funeral. People often gather at someone's house. They may prepare a meal for everyone to enjoy. Family and friends tell stories, talk about memories, cry, and even laugh. Others prefer to sit quietly and think about their loved one.

These are all normal reactions to the death of someone you love. Everyone must learn to live without that person. In time, it becomes easier. However, you'll probably always miss the person who passed away.

Glossary

afterlife: An existence after death.

cemetery: A place where the dead are buried.

ceremony: A formal act or series of acts performed in some regular way according to fixed rules.

gravestone: A stone monument placed over a grave, often with a name and dates carved into it.

grieve: To feel sorrow over the loss of something, especially a loved one.

honor: To show respect to someone.

procession: A group of people or cars moving forward in an orderly manner.

tradition: A way of thinking, behaving, or doing something that's been used by people in a particular society for a long time.

Index

Websites

Due to the changing nature of Internet links, PowerKids Press has developed an online list of websites related to the subject of this book. This site is updated regularly. Please use this link to access the list: www.powerkidslinks.com/help/funeral